New England Association of Railway Superintendents.

REPORT

OF THE

Trial of Locomotive Engines,

MADE UPON 1st and 2d OCTOBER, 1851.

BOSTON:
J. B. YERRINTON & SON, PRINTERS,
21 CORNHILL.
1852.

This Trial and resulting Report were made in connection with the Middlesex Mechanics' Association, in compliance with the following Circular, presented at a regular meeting of the Association: —

CIRCULAR EXTRA.

The Middlesex Mechanic Association, by their Committee of Arrangements for an exhibition of Improvements in the Mechanic Arts and Manufactured Articles, to be opened on the 6th of September, 1851, in the city of Lowell, respectfully invite the Agents and Superintendents of Railroads, and Manufacturers of Locomotives and Railroad Cars, to exhibit at the Fair some of their best Locomotive Engines, and Passenger and Merchandise Cars, for which suitable shelter will be provided by the Association, on Monday, the 29th of September next. This part of the Exhibition will be open for inspection on Tuesday, the 30th of September, and on the Wednesday and Thursday next following, there will be trials of speed on the Boston and Lowell Road, near Lowell; and of power and draught, on the disused track of the Boston and Maine Railroad, in Wilmington, between the Boston and Lowell and the Boston and Maine Roads. The Agent of the Boston and Lowell Railroad has kindly offered to furnish loaded cars for trial of power and draught, and also fuel ready prepared, charged at cost only. The fuel to be of an equal quality, so that, in this respect, no advantage may be had by one Locomotive over another.

The New England Association of Railroad Superintendents will nominate three judicious, disinterested persons, to be confirmed by the Government of the Middlesex Mechanic Association, to act as judges, and report upon this part of the Exhibition, on whose awards Medals and Diplomas will be issued and awarded by the Mechanic Association.

Any individuals or companies having in their possession any improvements, either patented or unpatented, of parts, parcels, or fixtures of any kind, appertaining to Railroads, Locomotives or Cars, are requested to exhibit them.

The project was approved of by this Association, and Messrs. WALDO HIGGINSON, L. TILTON and W. P. PARROTT were appointed a Committee, in behalf of this Association, to make the necessary arrangements for carrying out the plan suggested by the above circular, and this Committee sent the following circular to parties interested in this trial:—

At a recent meeting of the NEW ENGLAND ASSOCIATION OF RAILROAD SUPERINTENDENTS, the undersigned were appointed a Committee to confer with the Mechanics' Association of Lowell, in regard to a show and trial of Locomotive Engines, in connection with their general Exhibition, about to be held in that city. They are now able to announce that the Government of the Mechanics' Association has very liberally decided thus to extend its Exhibition, and that arrangements have been made for the safe keeping of Engines, and for a trial of their merits.

The undersigned would, therefore, add their invitation to that of the Mechanics' Association, and extend it to all Railroad Companies and Engine Builders, to send Locomotives to the proposed Exhibition.

The value of such examinations and comparisons as can be made on the occasion, is too obvious to require comment. The absolute results attained by actual performance on carefully described tracks, and with loads precisely ascertained, cannot fail to be highly interesting and serviceable.

A report upon this part of the Exhibition will be made in detail by a competent and disinterested tribunal, which is chosen by the Government of the Mechanics' Association, but which, at their request, will be nominated by the Association of Superintendents.

The undersigned would also unite with the Mechanics' Association of Lowell, in inviting, upon this occasion, a display of mechanical improvements, of any kind, appertaining to Railways.

WALDO HIGGINSON,
L. TILTON,
WM. P. PARROTT, } Committee.

Subsequently, all the arrangements were made by the Association, and the experiments and report made by the judges appointed, in accordance with the agreement.

As the trial was thus made in connection with this Association, and as the Report upon Railway apparatus of all kinds is of especial interest to the members, and others interested in Railway management, it was considered expedient, with the consent of the Executive Committee of the Mechanics' Association, to publish, in the present form, that part of theii general report which relates to Railway matters.

AGREEMENT OF THE JUDGES.

It has been agreed by the Judges to adopt the following method of experiment and record : —

The Engines entered for trial shall be recorded in detail, according to the form, a copy of which will be given to each of the Engineers.

FOR THE TRIAL OF SPEED.

The balances to be tested on all the Engines, and the result of the examination recorded.

The Engines to work as near 100 lbs. per square inch as may be, but may work at pressures between 80 and 120 pounds, if required ; the difference to be recorded, and the pressure to be maintained at the initial pressure, during the Experiment.

The load to be constant, and equal to six loaded passenger cars. The test to be by the speed with which the constant load is carried over a certain distance, said speed being corrected according to the weight of the Engines and pressure of steam.

FOR THE TRIAL OF POWER OF DRAUGHT.

The trials of power to be made with a constant load, and the difference of power in the Engines to be indicated by the difference of speed, to be corrected according to the dimensions of the Engines and pressure of the steam.

The formula by which the corrections noted above are to be made, will be agreed upon hereafter.

LOWELL, September 30th, 1851.

CLASS NO. 4.

LOCOMOTIVE ENGINES, RAILWAY CARRIAGES AND APPARATUS.

JUDGES:

Capt. WILLIAM H. SWIFT,	ISAAC HINCKLEY,
Prof. BENJAMIN PIERCE,	GEORGE H. CORLISS,

WILLIAM P. PARROTT.

To the Chairman of the Executive Committee of the Middlesex Mechanics' Association:

Sir,—The undersigned, appointed Judges for the Class No. 4, in the present Exhibition, having attended to their duties, respectfully submit the following report and awards.

We have to regret that the number of articles in our class is so limited; but trust that hereafter it may be increased to the amount which the great interest it represents demands.

The list of articles in the Fair marked in the Catalogue as belonging to Class No. 4 is as follows:

Nos. 1383, 1385, 1427, 1465, 1475, 1515.

To this list are to be added some articles and machines not on the Catalogue, nor in the halls of the Exhibition, viz.:

L. D. Livermore's patent car coupling, attached to two cars on the Boston and Lowell Railroad, and the following Locomotives, viz.:

Milo.—Freight Engine from Boston and Lowell Railroad Co.,—built by Hinckley and Drury. Rebuilt in 1851 by B. and L. R. R. Co. G. B. King, Master Machinist.

Addison Gilmore.—Passenger Engine from Western Railroad,—built in 1850–'51, by W. R. R. Co., at Springfield. Mr. Eddy, Master Machinist.

Neponset.—Passenger Engine from Boston and Providence R. R. Co.,—built at the shop of B. and P. R. R., 1849. G. S. Griggs, Master Machinist.

Highlander.—Freight Engine from Boston and Providence R. R. Co.,—built at their shop, in 1850. G. S. Griggs, Master Machinist.

Dedham.—Passenger Tank-Engine from Boston and Providence R. R. Co.,—built at their shop, in 1851. G. S. Griggs, Master Machinist.

Addison Gilmore.—Passenger Engine from Connecticut and Passumpsic R. R. Co.,—built in 1851, by Amoskeag Company, of Manchester, N. H. Oliver W. Bayley, Superintendent.

Nathan Hale.—Passenger Engine from Boston and Worcester R. R. Co.,—built in 1851, by Seth Wilmarth, Union Works, Boston.

Union.—Passenger Engine from Fitchburg R. R. Co.,—built in 1851, by Boston Locomotive Works.

St. Clair.—Freight Engine from Ogdensburgh R. R. Co.,—built at shop of Essex Co., Lawrence, in 1851. Caleb W. Marvel, Supt.

Essex.—Passenger Engine from Boston and Lowell R. R. Co.,—built in 1850, at shop of Essex Company, Lawrence. Caleb W. Marvel, Superintendent.

1383. Is a specimen of single plate car wheel, manufactured by C. Randlett & Co., Meredith Bridge, N. H. A well manufactured car wheel.

1385. Is a car wheel, from Levi B. Tyng, of Lowell, with its tire fastened in the mode patented by Mr. Perkins, late Master Machinist of the Baltimore and Ohio Railroad, and applicable to both cast or wrought tires. We approve of the principle which Mr. Tyng has adopted in the application of tires to railroad wheels, as the present mode of shrinking them on is objectionable, for obvious reasons.

The manner in which the tire is secured by this method, appears to us to be sufficient in strength and simple in construction. We recommend it to the attention of gentlemen engaged in railroad management.

1427. Cast car wheels, from the Brandon Car Wheel Co., Brandon, Vt.; John Howe, Jr., Agent. A good article.

Also, from the same manufactory, one pair of Mowry's self-acting car couplings.

We recommend this car coupling to the attention of railroad gentlemen, as its construction is such as to allow it to be used with the old couplings; and it combines the advantages of the self-acting coupling, and the simple pin and link now in use. It possesses, also, the advantage of being afforded at a low price, on account of its simplicity of construction. For these considerations, we have awarded to Mr. Mowry a Silver Medal, for the best car coupling.

1465. A railroad check signal, from Richard Hollings, Boston. This is an ingenious contrivance, but, in our opinion, not practically useful; as contrivances quite similar, and for the same purpose, have been frequently tried, but abandoned, as being useless.

1475. Lightner's patent car-box, from H. F. ALEXANDER, Boston. This invention and its merits are so well known to the managers of railroads, in this section of the country, that it requires no extended notice from us. In our opinion, it has well deserved the encomiums which it has received from those who have examined its merits heretofore.

1515. Livermore's patent coupling and truck guide, from S. D. LIVERMORE, Montpelier, Vt. This is an ingenious contrivance, for guiding the trucks of long railroad cars; and is now attached to two of the cars of the Boston and Lowell Railroad Co. We are unable to state precisely the advantages and disadvantages in its use, as more time would have been required to test it thoroughly, than we have had at our disposal. We saw it in practical use, over about twenty miles of the road, and it worked well. The advantages claimed are, that the wear and resistance upon curves are greatly reduced by its use, and the motion of the cars rendered more easy.

In this, as in other instances, we experience the great need of some instrument by which the resistances upon railroads might be measured with a proper degree of accuracy, without having recourse to experiments involving an expenditure of time and money, of large amount, to determine a point which might be determined in a few hours, with suitable means. We regret, for the sake of this ingenious inventor, that we had not such means at our disposal. We would recommend the examination of his plan, especially to parties about to furnish a road with cars, for it cannot conveniently be partially adopted, since cars built in accordance with it, cannot well be coupled with cars fitted with the common coupling.

REPORT ON LOCOMOTIVE ENGINES.

It gives us much pleasure to report, that this branch of Class No. 4 was well represented. The engines exhibited were few, as compared with the vast number now manufactured; but we believe that it would be difficult to surpass them in quality.

Another consideration worthy of notice is, that they were taken from every-day work, and were not built for the occasion. In this respect, the exhibition was a practical one.

In regard to workmanship, we could make no comparison, as many of the most important parts of such machines cannot be seen without taking them apart, which it was not convenient to do.

Where work is all of so good a quality as it was in this instance, there could be no real advantage gained, in deciding points of small difference. We have therefore concluded not to embrace this branch of the investigation in this report.

For the description of the engines, we refer to the table annexed, (marked 3,) in which the dimensions, as furnished us by the contributors, are given in detail.

In relation to the questions of proportions, and the arrangement of the machinery, we believe that these will be more satisfactorily indicated by the results of the trials, than by any description consistent with the limits of this report.

The trial of speed was made upon that part of the Boston and Lowell Railroad which lies between the 15th and 24th mile posts, numbering from Boston.

The rules adopted were—

1st. That all engines, upon this trial, should carry the same load over the same distance.

2d. That the pressure of steam in the boilers should not exceed one hundred and twenty, nor be less than seventy pounds, per square inch.

3d. That the pressure at starting should be taken as the pressure under which the engine worked over the whole distance; the safety valve balances remaining unaltered.

[The balances were tested, as far as practicable, by thermometers; and the results, (marked 5,) and a table, (marked 6,) for reducing them to pressure, are annexed to this report.]

The constant load, in the trial of speed, consisted (beside the tender) of six covered freight cars, each loaded with five tons, one long passenger car, and twenty-one passengers; the whole weighing eighty-five tons.

This constant load caused a displacement of 17,680 cubic feet of air; being in length, two hundred and twenty-one feet, height ten feet, width eight feet.

Each engine, with its train, started from the fifteenth mile post, at a given signal, and made its best time to the twenty-fourth mile post, where the observations terminated.

A detailed description of the track run over, (marked 1,) with a corresponding table (marked 4) of times at each station, is annexed, for the use of those who may wish to examine the matter in detail.

To reduce the observed time of running to the time in which the distance should have been run, consistently with the published terms, (viz. to reduce in proportion to the weight of the engine and pressure of steam,) it became necessary to adopt some formula by which this reduction could be made. We have not the means of proposing an exact formula for this purpose, as we have not at our command experiments upon which to base the necessary computations. We have therefore used an empirical formula, which we believe to be sufficiently accurate for the purposes of comparison; as the errors cannot amount to enough to involve injustice to either of the parties interested in the result. This formula is based upon the assumption, that an engine of 25 tons weight, under an effective pressure of 100 lbs. to the square inch, would, upon this track, without load other than the tender, run the observed distance, at the rate of eighty miles per hour, or in four hundred and five seconds.

This standard assumed, and the load and distance being constant, it is only requisite to apply the correction in time, due to the variable weights and pressures of the different engines.

For this purpose, the following proportion was used:—

$$1 : \left(\frac{2\,W\,P}{10.000.000}\right) - 1 :: t - 405'' : \text{correction},$$

(the correction being plus or minus, as $\frac{2\,W\,P}{10.000.000}$ is greater or less than unity.)

W, representing weight of engine in pounds; P, the effective pressure of steam in boiler, in pounds per square inch; t, the observed time, in seconds.

Following this formula, the results were obtained contained in table marked (7.)

It will be noticed, upon comparison, that the reduced times follow generally in order with the observed times, after the proper corrections for differences of weight and pressure have been made.

We have confidence that equal justice has been done to all, with the exception of the Addison Gilmore, of the Connecticut and Passumpsic River Railroad.

This engine was worked at a much higher pressure than the others, and thus would, under equal circumstances, have had a decided advantage; but as she had just come from the shop, and never before been attached to a train, it is difficult, if not impossible, to arrive at a correct estimate of her power, as compared with the others; to which is to be added the consideration, that she was worked at a pressure above that proposed by the published rules.

We have given the results of the trial of this engine, but have not included it as competing for a prize, since it did not come within the prescribed rules.

The Dedham, a small tank-engine, built by G. S. Griggs, of the Boston and Providence Railroad, was run over the same track, on the day after the trial of the other passenger engines, with a load of two passenger cars and eighty-one passengers, making an entire weight of eighteen tons.

The time in which this engine passed over the nine miles, is given in detail with the others; but with such a disproportioned load, we think it inexpedient, with our present means of judging, to make any comparison.

We regret this, as we believe that, on many of our roads, engines of this class must be introduced, for economical reasons, before full accommodation can be given to the public, or remuneration to the stockholders.

The trial of the Freight Engines was made upon the branch track connecting the Boston and Lowell Railroad and the Boston and Maine Railroad at Wilmington, over a distance of nine thousand one hundred feet in length. The load consisted of one hundred and fourteen loaded cars, estimated to weigh, cars included, six hundred and fifty tons.

Each engine first backed this train down to the starting point, which was at the top of an inclined plane of fourteen feet to the mile; and from this point they started, at a given signal, making their best time to the point at the other extremity of the branch.

For the details of this track, we refer to the statement annexed to this report, (marked 2,) with the corresponding table of times, as in the trial of speed, in table (marked 4.)

For the reduction of these engines, we have used the same formula as in the preceding case; with the exceptions, that the standard time is taken at one hundred and forty-four seconds, instead of four hundred and five seconds, and the pressure shown by the balances, instead of the effective pressure.

The limited time we had to prepare for these experiments, must be our excuse for their being so incomplete in detail and arrangement; and the want of direct experiment, to determine the basis upon which to ground absolute formulas, prevented us from making more than a comparative statement of the performances of the engines of both classes.

We take the liberty of expressing our regret, that so great a deficiency exists in our knowledge in this department of railroad management.

The power now applied for the purpose of transportation on railroads is very large, and upon its proper application depends, in a great degree, the success of this great interest in this section.

It is apparent, even to a casual observer, that the railroads have increased in a greater ratio than the amount of business they can have to do. It becomes, therefore, of vital importance, that the greatest possible saving should be made in all the details of working and maintenance; and in the case under consideration, that the weight of the engines should be reduced, and their power increased, to the greatest limit consistent with the proper durability of the machines.

We trust that this experiment will be followed up by those interested, until a series of observations, properly made, may enable railroad managers to judge with certainty, having actual, and not theoretical knowledge, for their guide.

It was our intention to have prepared instruments for the purpose of measuring the power of draught directly; and also certain apparatus for testing the steadiness with which the machines run upon the track.

Some progress was made, but we were unable to get them completed in season for use. Should they be wanted for future experiments, it will take probably but a short time to perfect them.

We present our thanks to the officers and men of the Boston and Lowell Railroad, for the prompt and ample assistance rendered by them, in accommodating the engines brought to Lowell for exhibition; and for the skill and care with which the arrangements were made for running the experimental trains, no accident or delay having occurred.

We are also indebted to Messrs. Newell, Haeffely, and Harris, Civil Engineers, for their assistance in noting the times and distances run by the engines, to Messrs. Perrin and Winslow for testing the balances of the engines by thermometers introduced into the steam, and to Messrs. Cheney and Harris for aid in recording notes during the trial.

In conclusion, we indulge in the hope, that these experiments may be the commencement of a series, which will ultimately lead to a more perfect knowledge of the capabilities of the locomotive engine; and in practice, to a greater economy of power in working this important machine.

The comparison of these experiments with those made in England in 1830–'31, will show the great increase of speed already attained, as compared with the weight of the engine and the load carried; and will be an incentive to further improvement.

AWARDS.

In awarding the Medals, we have in all cases made the awards to the persons or Companies contributing; for we had no means of ascertaining to whom the merits of the articles, or Machines, were fairly due. We would, however, respectfully recommend, in event of the confirmation of our awards, that the parties, to whom Medals are given, should be consulted in regard to the inscription to be engraved upon each.

To JOHN HOWE, JR., Agent of the Brandon Works, a Silver Medal, for Mowry's Car Coupling.

To the ADDISON GILMORE, from the Western Railroad, a Gold Medal, for the best time made.

To the NATHAN HALE, Boston and Worcester Railroad, a Silver Medal, for the second best time made.

To the DEDHAM, from the Boston and Providence Railroad, for the peculiar arrangement of the engine and tender, the importance of which we have alluded to; and for the drawing apparatus, which increases the adhesion with increased load, or increased draught on inclined planes, a Silver Medal.

To the MILO, freight engine, from the Boston and Lowell Railroad, for the best performance according to the prescribed rules, a Gold Medal.

To the ST. CLAIR, freight engine, from the Ogdensburgh Railroad, for the second best performance, a Silver Medal.

By order of the Board of Judges of Class No. 4,

WM. P. PARROTT,

For the Committee.

LOWELL, October 18th, 1851.

(TABLE 1.)

BOSTON AND LOWELL RAILROAD,

As staked out for trial of speed of Locomotives upon October 1st, 1851, commencing at 15th Mile Post, numbered from Boston.

To		Feet.	Curves	Tangents	Ellipse
1	Straight,	1663		1663	
2	Curve R. 3000 feet,	809	809		
3	Straight to change of grade,	464			
4	" to 16th mile post,	2344			
5	" to tangential point,	1183		3991	
6	Curve R. 3000 feet " "	825	825		
7	Straight to change of grade,	2228			
8	" to 17th mile post,	1044			
9	" to tangential point,	1130		4402	
10	Curve R. 3000 feet, " "	420	420		
11	Straight to change of grade,	1517			
12	" to 18th mile post,	2213			
13	" to 19th mile post,	5280			
14	" to change of grade,	2297			
15	" to tangential point and change of grade,	2799		14106	
16	Curve R. 3005.7 feet to change of grade,	100			
17	" " " to 20th mile post,	84			
18	" " " to tangential point,	1014	1198		
19	Ellipse,	306			306
20	Curve R. 3000 feet to tangential point,	1197	1197		
21	Straight " " " "	902		902	
22	Curve R. 3063.5 to 21st mile post,	1861			
23	" " " to change of grade,	2152			
24	" " " to tangential point,	783	4796		
25	Straight to change of grade,	150			
26	" " " "	200			
27	" " " 22d mile post,	1995			
28	" " change of grade,	560			
29	" " " " " .	2404			
30	" to tangential point and change of grade,	1875		7184	
31	Curve R. 3671.5 to 23d mile post,	441			
32	" " " to tangential point and change of grade,	2062	2503		
33	Straight to " " "	897		897	
34	Curve R. 3000 ft. to " "	631	631		
35	Straight to 24th mile post,	1690		1690	
		47520	12379	34835	306

GRADIENTS.

	At rate of per mile in feet.	No. of feet.
Ascend'g	8,2368	2936
"	4,4352	6580
Level		4111
Ascend'g	4,0128	9790
Level		2799
Ascend'g	4,2200	100
"	9,5040	7516
Level		933
Ascend'g	4,2200	200
Level		2555
Descend.	7,1800	2404
"	7,4980	1875
"	7,0650	2503
"	7,0000	897
"	,0300	2321
		47520

(TABLE 2.)

For trial of Draught of Locomotives on the Wilmington Branch Railroad, the engine stood at station 106. From thence toward the Boston and Maine Railroad, the grade is down $13\frac{73}{100}$ feet per mile, for 1400 feet; and thence level, 400 feet.

From station 106, toward the Boston and Lowell Railroad, the grade is down, $19\frac{85}{100}$ feet per mile, 2100 feet; then level, 500 feet; then up, $9\frac{45}{100}$ feet per mile, 1000 feet; then up, $5\frac{28}{100}$ feet per mile, 1000 feet; then up, $3\frac{17}{100}$ feet per mile, 1000 feet; then level, 1000 feet; then up, $6\frac{86}{100}$ feet per mile, 1000 feet; then up, $3\frac{96}{100}$ feet per mile, 2000 feet.

From station 106, toward the Boston and Lowell Railroad, straight, 5447 feet; then curved, with a radius of 6720 feet, 688 feet; then straight to the last station.

1	64	feet from starting point,————		17th Mile Post.
2	2036	"	to Station 85	
3	1500	"	" " 70	
4	1000	"	" " 60	
5	707	"	" " $52\frac{93}{100}$————	16th Mile Post.
6	140	"	" Tangent Point.	
7	688	"	" " "	
8	465	"	" " 40	
9	1000	"	" " 30	
10	1000	"	" " 20	
11	500	"	" " 15	

(TABLE 3.)

TABLE OF DIMENSIONS OF THE LOCOMOTIVES

ENTERED FOR TRIAL OF SPEED AND DRAUGHT (AS FURNISHED BY CONTRIBUTORS.)

NAMES OF ENGINES.	Cylinder connections.	Diameter of Cylinder.	Length of Stroke.	Diameter of Boiler.	Length of Boiler.	Number of Tubes.	Length of Tubes.	Diameter of Tubes.	Area exposed to contact of heated air.	Length of Fire Box.	Width of ditto.	Height above Grate-bars of ditto.	Fire surface of ditto.	Total effective Fire surface.	Area of Grate.	Diameter of Chimney.	Height of Chimney above Smoke arch.	Height of Chimney above rail.	Steam Pipe.	Induction Ports.	Eduction Ports.	Diameter of Blast Pipe.	Diameter of Pump.	Length of Stroke.	No. of Driving Wheels.	Diameter of ditto.	No. of Carrying Wheels.	Diameter of ditto.	Diameter of Truck Wheels.	Weight of Engine in Working Trim.	Ditto Empty.
		Inch.	In	Inch.	Ft.In		Ft.In	In	Ft.	Ft.In	Ft.In	Ft.In	Feet.		Ft.	In	Ft.In	Ft.In	In.	Inches.	Inch.	Inch.	In	In		Ft.In		Ft.In	Ft.In	Lbs.	
Milo, ...	Outsi'e	13½	20	38	11.2½	88	10.8	2		2.10	3.2	3.7½				14	5.7	13.3	5x1¼	7¼x1¼	7¼x1¼	1¾	2¼	7	6	4.0	0			38900	
Addison Gilmore, (W. R. R.)	Outsi'e	15⅜	26	50	12.4	196	12.4	1¾	1104	3.8½	3.		68	1172	11⅜		8.0	16.0		10x1.3-16		3¼			2	6.9	2	4.6	2.6	50885	
Neponset, . . .	Inside,	14¾	20	43x41	11.	123	11.	2	620	2.11	3.2	4.3	59	679	9½	14	5.6	13.6	3¾	9x1	9x2	2½	1⅝	20	4	5.6	0		2.6	43776	
Highlander,	Inside,	14¾	18	44	9.	142	9.	1¾	530	4.8	3.2	4.4	59	589	8½	14	6.0	13.2	3¾	9x1	9x2	2⅓	1⅝	18	6	4.0	0		0.0	40015	
Dedham, . . .	Inside,	9	16	30	8.	115	8.	1½	331	1.8	2.8	3.1	22	363	4½	10	7.6	13.3	3	7x¾	7x1¾	1½	1¼	16	2	4.6	0		2.9	25350	
Addison Gilmore, (C. & P. R. R.)	In ide,	16	20	42	11.	150	11.	2		3.5	3.6	5.6				14	4.6	13.7	3	12x1⅓	12x2	2¼	2½	7	4	6.6	0		2.6	46320	
Nathan Hale, . .	Inside,	16	20	42½	11.	118	11.	1⅞	637	3.6½	3.2½	4.10	58.1-9	695.1-6	10⅔	15	4.4	13.0	5	12x1¾	12x2½	2¼	3½	5	4	5.6	0		2.6	47095	
Union, ...	Inside,	16	20		10.6	125	10.6	2		3.	3.2	4.6			9½	14	5.6	13.5	3	11x1¾	11x2	2¼	2¾	8	4	5.6	0		2.6	46990	
St. Clair, . . .	Inside,	15	20	42	10.10	153		1¾	694	3.4½	3.2½	4.3	66.1-18	760	10¾	15	5.0	12.6	3¾	11x1.1-16	11x2	2.3-16	2¾	6½	4	4.6	0			48650	
Essex, ...	Inside,	15	20	42	10.10	139		1¾	630	3.4½	3.2½	3.10	61.3-10	691.½	10¾	15	5.0	13.3	3¾	11x1.1-16	11x2	2⅛	2¾	6½	2	6.0	2	4.6		48470	44200

These dimensions were furnished by the Contributors. It is regretted that in some instances the schedules are deficient.

(TABLE 5.)

LOWELL, October 2, 1851.

TO MESSRS. W. P. PARROTT AND OTHERS,
Committee on the performance of Locomotive Engines:

GENTLEMEN,—The undersigned being requested to compare the spring balance scales attached to the several safety valves of the following Locomotives, with the Mercurial gauge, would respectfully submit the following result:—

Name of Engines.	*Spring Scale.*			
ADDISON GILMORE, Built by Amoskeag Manufacturing Co.	144	equal to	354° :	of heat.
NEPONSET, Built by Boston and Providence R. R. Co.	100	"	338° :	"
ADDISON GILMORE, Built by Western Railroad Co.	100	"	329° :	"
NATHAN HALE, Built by S. Wilmarth, Union Works,	110	"	339° :	"
ESSEX,	100	"	340° :	"

Respectfully submitted, &c.,

P. I. PERRIN,
JOHN B. WINSLOW.

(TABLE 6.)

Table of the Volume of Steam generated under different Pressures, compared to the Volume of Water that has produced it.

Compiled by COMTE DE PAMBOUR. See "Theory of the Steam Engine," by that Author.

Total pressure in English pounds per square inch.	Corresponding Temperature by Fahrenheit's Thermometer. Degrees—Deci'l.	Volume of the steam compared to the volume of the water that has produced it.	Total pressure in English pounds per square inch.	Corresponding Temperature by Fahrenheit's Thermometer. Degrees—Deci'l.	Vol. of the steam compared to the volume of the water that has produced it.
1	102.9	20954	41 56	289.6	498
2	126.1	10907	42 57	290.7	490
3	141.0	7455	43 58	291.9	482
4	152.3	5695	44 59	293.0	474
5	161.4	4624	45 60	294.1	467
6	169.2	3901	46 61	294.9	460
7	176.0	3380	47 62	295.9	453
8	182.0	2985	48 63	297.0	447
9	187.4	2676	49 64	298.1	440
10	192.4	2427	50 65	299.1	334
11	197.0	2222	51 66	300.1	428
12	201.3	2050	52 67	301.2	422
13	205.3	1903	53 68	302.2	417
14	209.0	1777	54 69	303.2	411
0 15	213.0	1669	55 70	304.2	406
1 16	216.4	1572	56 71	305.1	401
2 17	219.6	1487	57 72	306.1	396
3 18	222.6	1410	58 73	307.1	391
4 19	225.6	1342	59 74	308.0	386
5 20	228.3	1280	60 75	308.9	381
6 21	231.0	1224	61 76	309.9	377
7 22	233.6	1172	62 77	310.8	372
8 23	236.1	1125	63 78	311.7	368
9 24	238.4	1082	64 79	312.6	364
10 25	240.7	1042	65 80	313.5	359
11 26	243.0	1005	66 81	314.3	355
12 27	245.1	971	67 82	315.2	351
13 28	247.2	939	68 83	316.1	348
14 29	249.2	909	69 84	316.9	344
15 30	251.2	882	70 85	317.8	340
16 31	253.1	855	71 86	318.6	337
17 32	255.0	831	72 87	319.4	333
18 33	256.8	808	73 88	320.3	330
19 34	258.6	786	74 89	321.1	326
20 35	260.3	765	75 90	321.9	323
21 36	262.0	746	76 91	322.7	320
22 37	263.7	727	77 92	323.5	317
23 38	265.3	710	78 93	324.3	313
24 39	266.9	693	79 94	325.0	310
25 40	268.4	677	80 95	325.8	307
26 41	269.9	662	81 96	326.6	305
27 42	271.4	647	82 97	327.3	302
28 43	272.9	634	83 98	328.1	299
29 44	274.3	620	84 99	328.8	296
30 45	275.7	608	85 100	329.6	293
31 46	277.1	596	90 105	333.2	281
32 47	278.4	584	105 120	343.3	249
33 48	279.7	573	120 135	352.4	224
34 49	281.0	562	135 150	360.8	203
35 50	282.3	552	150 165	368.5	187
36 51	283.6	542	165 180	375.6	173
37 52	284.8	532	180 195	382.3	161
38 53	286.0	523	195 210	388.6	150
39 54	287.2	514	210 225	394.6	141
40 55	288.4	506	225 240	400.2	133

The table of the "Volume of Steam" shows directly how many cubic feet of steam, at the corresponding temperature and pressure, is formed from one cubic foot of water: per example—Take 58 lbs. per square inch, the steam at this pressure will be as 482 to 1; or one cubic foot of water will make 482 cubic feet of steam, at that pressure.

TABLE (7.)

TABLE OF RESULTS OF TRIALS WITH LOCOMCTIVES,

ON THE BOSTON AND LOWELL RAILROAD, OCT. 1st and 2d, 1851.

TRIALS OF SPEED.

NAME OF ENGINE.	Weight in pounds.	Effecti'e pressure of pounds to a square inch.	Weight x 2.	Wt. x 2 x pressure / 10.000.000	Observed time.	Correction.	Corrected time.
Addison Gilmore (W)	50,885	84	101770	,8548680	738.2″	—48.3″	689.9″=11′.29.9″
Nathan Hale, ...	47,095	99	94190	,9324810	775.3″	—25″.	750.3″=12′.30.3″
Union, ...	46,990	97	93980	,9116060	847.6″	—39″.	808.6″=13′.28.6″
Neponset, ...	43,775	97	87550	,8492350	876.4″	—71″.	805″. =13′.25″.
Addison Gilmore (M)	46,320	124	92640	1,1487360	805.9″	+59.6″	865.5″=14′.25.5″
Essex, ...	48,470	100	96940	,9694000	888″	—14.8″	873.2″=14′.33.2″

TRIALS OF DRAUGHT.

		Lbs. pressure to sq. in. by scale.					
Milo, ...	38,900	120	77800	,9336000	678″	—35.5″	642.5″=10′.42.5″
St. Clair, ...	48,650	115	97300	1,1189500	601″	+54.3″	654.3′=10′.54.3″
Highlander, ...	40,015	120	80030	,9603600	784″	—25.4″	758.6″=12′.38.6″

www.ingramcontent.com/pod-product-compliance
Lightning Source LLC
LaVergne TN
LVHW020637110826
845149LV00004B/1254